Presidio House

Caleño Slang for Brave Foreigners

Cali / Valle del Cauca Edition

Presidio House LLC 2026

ISBN-13: 979-8-9951420-3-4

First Edition

Disclaimer

This book is a non-fiction educational and cultural guide to authentic colloquial Colombian Spanish. It contains real slang expressions used in everyday speech across different regions of Colombia, including informal, vulgar, strong, or regionally specific language that may be considered offensive, crude, or inappropriate in formal settings. All content is presented solely for linguistic, cultural, and educational purposes to help readers understand and communicate more naturally with native speakers.

The author and publisher do not endorse or encourage the use of profane, vulgar, or disrespectful language. Reader discretion is advised, especially for younger audiences or in professional/educational environments.

Welcome from La Vecina

¡Bienvenidos al mundo caleño, mi amor! Soy la Vecina de Cali — la que te recibe con un abrazo, un beso en la mejilla y un "chévere, mi rey". Aquí todo tiene ritmo, todo se baila, todo se goza. Tú vas a aprender a saludar con cariño, a aprobar con swing y a no perder el paso en la rumba más caliente del mundo. ¡Esto es Cali puro, con sabor a salsa y corazón grande! A mover las caderas, que la vida se vive bailando.

English Welcome

Welcome to the Caleño World, my love! I'm your Cali Vecina — the one who greets you with a hug, a kiss on the cheek, and a "chévere, my king." Here everything has rhythm, everything is danced, everything is enjoyed. You're going to learn how to greet with affection, approve with swing, and never miss a beat in the hottest party city in the world. This is pure Cali — with salsa flavor and a big heart! Let's move those hips, because life is meant to be danced.

How to Use This Book

Each entry is set up the same way so you can jump in fast and start sounding caleño right away:

Phrase – the exact Caleño slang expression you're going to use

Vecina – that's me breaking it down in my warm, rhythmic Cali voice

Meaning – the clear English sense and the real vibe behind it

Example – a real-life sentence the way we actually say it on the streets of Cali

Translation – the natural English version so you catch every bit of sabor

Say them out loud with swing and a smile, mi amor. Caleño slang is all about rhythm, flow, and that big heart. ¡A mover el esqueleto! You've got this.

Table of Contents

Saludos Caleños con Cariño y Swing

Caleño Greetings with Affection and Swing

(Entries 1–10)

Entry 1

¿Qué más, mi rey / mi reina?

Vecina:

Tú sueltas esto y ya estás hablando como un caleño de verdad — con cariño, con swing y ese toque de realeza que usamos para que la gente se sienta bienvenida desde el primer segundo.

Meaning:

Warm Caleño greeting meaning "what's up, my king / my queen?"

Example:

¿Qué más, mi rey? ¿Listo pa' gozar o qué?

Translation:

What's up, my king? Ready to enjoy or what?

Entry 2

¿Cómo estás, papi / mami?

Vecina:

Papi y mami salen naturales en Cali, hasta con amigos — tú lo dices con una sonrisa y la gente te responde como si ya fueras parte del parche.

Meaning:

Affectionate greeting meaning "how you doing, handsome / beautiful?"

Example:

¿Cómo estás, mami? Se te ve el swing hoy.

Translation:

How you doing, beautiful? You've got the swing today.

Entry 3

¿Todo chévere?

Vecina:

Chévere es la palabra estrella en Cali — tú la usas y ya estás chequeando si todo está rico, con ritmo y sin complicaciones.

Meaning:

Classic Caleño check meaning "everything cool / great?"

Example:

¿Todo chévere? Porque yo estoy que bailo solo.

Translation:

Everything cool? Because I'm ready to dance alone.

Entry 4

¿Qué hubo, mi amor?

Vecina:

Mi amor sale natural en Cali, hasta con desconocidos — tú lo dices y la gente te responde con una sonrisa porque ya te sientes como de la familia.

Meaning:

Loving greeting meaning "what's up, my love?"

Example:

¿Qué hubo, mi amor? ¿Vamos a mover el esqueleto?
Translation:
What's up, my love? Shall we move the skeleton?

Entry 5
¿Cómo va ese flow?
Vecina:
Flow es ritmo, es baile, es vida caleña — tú lo preguntas y ya estás invitando al otro a que te cuente cómo va su energía.
Meaning:
Rhythmic greeting meaning "how's that flow / vibe going?"
Example:
¿Cómo va ese flow? Porque aquí la cosa está sabrosa.
Translation:
How's that flow going? Because things are tasty here.

Entry 6
¿Todo sabroso?
Vecina:
Sabroso es gozar, disfrutar, vivir con sabor — tú lo dices y la gente te responde con swing porque en Cali todo tiene que sentirse rico.
Meaning:
Joyful check meaning "everything tasty / enjoyable?"
Example:
¿Todo sabroso? Se siente el ritmo en el aire.
Translation:

Everything tasty? You can feel the rhythm in the air.

Entry 7
¿Qué más, mi gente?
Vecina:
Mi gente es familia, es barrio, es Cali entero — tú lo sueltas y ya estás hablando con todo el mundo como si ya fueras parte del parche.
Meaning:
Warm group greeting meaning "what's up, my people?"
Example:
¿Qué más, mi gente? Hoy se goza con todo.
Translation:
What's up, my people? Today we enjoy everything.

Entry 8
¿Listo pa' gozar?
Vecina:
En Cali siempre estamos listos pa' gozar — tú lo preguntas y ya estás invitando a la rumba, porque aquí la vida se vive bailando.
Meaning:
Party-ready greeting meaning "ready to enjoy / party?"
Example:
¿Listo pa' gozar? Porque la rumba ya arrancó.
Translation:
Ready to enjoy? Because the party already started.

Entry 9

¿Cómo está el ambiente?

Vecina:

Ambiente es todo — música, gente, sabor — tú lo preguntas y ya estás chequeando si el lugar tiene ese swing caleño que buscamos.

Meaning:

Vibe check meaning "how's the atmosphere?"

Example:

¿Cómo está el ambiente? Se siente rico hoy.

Translation:

How's the atmosphere? Feels nice today.

Entry 10

¿Todo en salsa?

Vecina:

En salsa, en ritmo, en goce caleño — tú lo dices y ya estás invitando a que todo fluya con música y corazón, puro Cali.

Meaning:

Playful check meaning "everything in salsa / rhythm?"

Example:

¿Todo en salsa? Porque yo ya estoy bailando.

Translation:

Everything in salsa? Because I'm already dancing.

Aprobación con Sabor y Ritmo

Approval with Sabor and Rhythm
(Entries 11–20)

Entry 11
De una, mi amor
Vecina:
Tú dices "de una" y ya estás dentro — sin pensarlo dos veces, con todo el corazón caleño que dice "vamos pa'lante, mi amor".
Meaning:
Right away, my love / instantly
Example:
¿Vamos? De una, mi amor, yo te sigo.
Translation:
We going? Right away, my love — I'll follow you.

Entry 12
Eso está sabrosísimo
Vecina:
Cuando algo te encanta de verdad, "sabrosísimo" es la forma más caleña de decirlo — tú lo sueltas y la gente te responde con sonrisa y swing.
Meaning:
That's super tasty / incredibly enjoyable
Example:

El plan está sabrosísimo, vamos a gozar.
Translation:
The plan is super tasty — let's enjoy it.

Entry 13
Chévere, dale
Vecina:
Chévere y dale juntos es aprobación con ritmo — tú lo dices y ya estás dando luz verde con ese flow caleño que invita a moverse.
Meaning:
Cool, go ahead / let's do it
Example:
¿Lo hacemos? Chévere, dale que sí.
Translation:
We doing it? Cool, go ahead — yes.

Entry 14
Eso quedó rico
Vecina:
Cuando algo sale bien y sabe a triunfo, "eso quedó rico" es la forma más sabrosa de celebrarlo — tú lo usas y la gente siente el sabor del momento.
Meaning:
That turned out delicious / great
Example:
El baile quedó rico, qué nivel.
Translation:

The dance turned out great — what a level.

Entry 15
Me encanta
Vecina:
Me encanta sale del alma en Cali — tú lo dices con sentimiento y la gente sabe que estás aprobando con todo el corazón y el swing.
Meaning:
I love it
Example:
Me encanta el plan, vamos con todo.
Translation:
I love the plan — let's go all in.

Entry 16
Está divino
Vecina:
Cuando algo está perfecto y te hace sonreír, "está divino" es la forma más elegante y caleña de decirlo — tú lo sueltas y ya estás invitando a gozar.
Meaning:
It's divine / perfect
Example:
El parche está divino, pura buena energía.
Translation:
The hangout is divine — pure good energy.

Entry 17
Va con swing
Vecina:
Cuando algo fluye con ritmo y estilo, "va con swing" es la aprobación más caleña — tú lo dices y la gente sabe que estás sintiendo el groove.
Meaning:
Going with swing / rhythm
Example:
El proyecto va con swing, qué rico.
Translation:
The project is going with swing — so nice.

Entry 18
Eso pinta sabroso
Vecina:
Cuando algo promete goce total, "pinta sabroso" es la forma más rica de crear expectativa — tú lo usas y ya estás armando el plan con sabor.
Meaning:
That looks tasty / promising
Example:
Esa rumba pinta sabroso, hay que ir.
Translation:
That party looks tasty — we gotta go.

Entry 19
De una, vamos
Vecina:

De una y vamos juntos es pura disposición caleña — tú lo sueltas y ya estás moviendo el esqueleto sin esperar ni un segundo más.

Meaning:

Right away, let's go

Example:

¿Listos? De una, vamos pa' la pista.

Translation:

Ready? Right away — let's hit the dance floor.

Entry 20

Eso está al pelo

Vecina:

Cuando algo está justo perfecto, "está al pelo" es la aprobación más precisa y sabrosa — tú lo dices y la gente sabe que todo cuadró con swing.

Meaning:

Just right / spot on

Example:

El ritmo está al pelo, a bailar.

Translation:

The rhythm is spot on — let's dance.

Emoción con Ritmo y Corazón

Emotions with Rhythm and Heart

(Entries 21–30)

Entry 21

Estoy que me derrito

Vecina:

When the excitement or the heat is too much and you're melting on the inside, "estoy que me derrito" is the caleño way to say it — you'll drop this and everyone will smile because they feel the same fire.

Meaning:

I'm melting / overwhelmed with excitement

Example:

Con esa salsa estoy que me derrito, qué rico.

Translation:

With that salsa I'm melting — so good.

Entry 22

Me tiene loco/a

Vecina:

When something has you wild with joy and you can't hide it, "me tiene loco/a" is how we say it's driving us crazy in the best way — you'll use this and the whole room will feel your energy.

Meaning:

It's driving me crazy / wild with excitement

Example:

El parche me tiene loco, no puedo parar.

Translation:

The hangout is driving me crazy — I can't stop.

Entry 23

Estoy en otra dimensión

Vecina:

When the moment is so good you're on a whole different level, "estoy en otra dimensión" is the caleño way to say you're floating — you'll say it and people will know you're living the vibe.

Meaning:

I'm in another dimension / next-level joy

Example:

Con esta música estoy en otra dimensión.

Translation:

With this music I'm in another dimension.

Entry 24

Me voló la cabeza

Vecina:

When something hits you so hard it leaves you speechless, "me voló la cabeza" is how we say it blew our minds — you'll use this on the dance floor and everyone will want the story.

Meaning:

That blew my mind

Example:
El paso que se mandó me voló la cabeza.
Translation:
The move he pulled blew my mind.

Entry 25
Estoy embalado/a
Vecina:
When you're fully locked into the moment and can't stop, "estoy embalado/a" is the caleño way to say you're deep in it — you'll sound like you're living the rhythm.
Meaning:
I'm fully into it / accelerated
Example:
Estoy embalada con esta rumba, no paro.
Translation:
I'm fully into this party — I don't stop.

Entry 26
Me tiene prendido/a
Vecina:
When the energy has you lit from the inside, "me tiene prendido/a" is how we say the fire is on — you'll drop this and the whole group will feel the heat.
Meaning:
It's got me lit / fired up
Example:
La salsa me tiene prendida, vamos a bailar.
Translation:

The salsa has me lit — let's dance.

Entry 27
Estoy que exploto
Vecina:
When the joy is about to burst out of you, "estoy que exploto" is the caleño way to say you're exploding with happiness — you'll say it with a big smile and the party will follow.
Meaning:
I'm about to burst / exploding
Example:
Estoy que exploto con esta energía.
Translation:
I'm about to burst with this energy.

Entry 28
Me tiene feliz
Vecina:
When something puts a real smile on your face, "me tiene feliz" is the warm caleño way to say you're happy — you'll use this and everyone will feel the good vibe.
Meaning:
It's got me happy / smiling big
Example:
El plan me tiene feliz, qué sabroso.
Translation:
The plan has me happy — so tasty.

Entry 29
Estoy volando
Vecina:
When the music or the moment lifts you up, "estoy volando" is how we say you're flying — you'll say it on the dance floor and people will know you're in the zone.
Meaning:
I'm flying / high
Example:
Con esa pareja estoy volando en la pista.
Translation:
With that partner I'm flying on the dance floor.

Entry 30
Me tiene bailando por dentro
Vecina:
When the rhythm is moving inside you even if you're standing still, "me tiene bailando por dentro" is the sweetest caleño way to say you're thrilled — you'll use this and the whole room will feel it.
Meaning:
It's got me dancing inside / thrilled
Example:
La canción me tiene bailando por dentro.
Translation:
The song has me dancing inside.

Rumba Caleña que se Baila con el Alma

Caleño Rumba That You Dance with Your Soul
(Entries 31–40)

Entry 31
Se armó la rumba
Vecina:
When the musicians show up and the night suddenly comes alive, "se armó la rumba" is how we say the party just kicked off — you'll drop this and the whole room will feel the Cali heat.
Meaning:
The party kicked off
Example:
Llegaron los músicos y se armó la rumba.
Translation:
The musicians arrived and the party kicked off.

Entry 32
Esto está sabrosísimo
Vecina:
When the rumba is so good your whole body wants to move, "esto está sabrosísimo" is the caleño way to say the night just got delicious — you'll use this and everyone will smile because they feel it too.

Meaning:
This is super tasty / incredibly enjoyable
Example:
La rumba está sabrosísima, no paramos.
Translation:
The party is super tasty — we don't stop.

Entry 33
Se prendió la pista
Vecina:
When the dance floor suddenly lights up and everyone starts moving, "se prendió la pista" is how we announce the fire has started — you'll say it and the energy will jump.
Meaning:
The dance floor lit up
Example:
Se prendió la pista con esa salsa vieja.
Translation:
The dance floor lit up with that old-school salsa.

Entry 34
Esto está con swing
Vecina:
When the vibe has that perfect Cali groove, "esto está con swing" is the rhythmic way we say it's flowing right — you'll use this and people will know you're feeling the sabor.
Meaning:

This has swing / rhythm

Example:

El ambiente está con swing, qué rico.

Translation:

The vibe has swing — so nice.

Entry 35

Se armó el goce

Vecina:

When the real enjoyment explodes, "se armó el goce" is how we say the fun has officially begun — you'll drop this and the whole group will feel the Cali joy.

Meaning:

The enjoyment kicked off

Example:

Con esa pareja se armó el goce.

Translation:

With that partner the enjoyment kicked off.

Entry 36

Esto está caliente

Vecina:

When the party is burning with passion and heat, "esto está caliente" is the caleño way to say it's on fire — you'll say it and the dance floor will answer back.

Meaning:

This is hot / intense

Example:

La rumba está caliente, no hay quien pare.

Translation:
The party is hot — no one's stopping.

Entry 37
Aquí se goza
Vecina:
Here we enjoy everything with heart and rhythm — you'll say "aquí se goza" and people will know you already understand the Cali way of living.
Meaning:
Here we enjoy / dance / live
Example:
Aquí se goza con todo, pura salsa.
Translation:
Here we enjoy everything — pure salsa.

Entry 38
Esto está divino
Vecina:
When the night feels perfect and full of sabor, "esto está divino" is the elegant caleño way to say it's heavenly — you'll use this and the vibe will rise even higher.
Meaning:
This is divine / perfect
Example:
El ambiente está divino, vamos a bailar.
Translation:
The vibe is divine — let's dance.

Entry 39

La cosa está rica

Vecina:

When everything feels tasty and worth enjoying, "la cosa está rica" is how we say the night is delicious — you'll drop this and the whole room will agree with a smile.

Meaning:

The situation is tasty / great

Example:

La cosa está rica, no hay que parar.

Translation:

Things are tasty — no need to stop.

Entry 40

Se puso bueno

Vecina:

When the party reaches that sweet spot after the warm-up, "se puso bueno" is the caleño way to say it just got really good — you'll say it and the hips will answer.

Meaning:

It got really good

Example:

Después del break se puso bueno el parche.

Translation:

After the break the hangout got really good.

Plata & Flow que se Mueve con Estilo

Money & Flow That Moves with Style
(Entries 41–50)

Entry 41
Estoy seco/a
Vecina:
When your pockets are empty but your style is still on point, "estoy seco/a" is the caleño way to say you're broke — you'll drop this with a smile and the rumba keeps going anyway.
Meaning:
I'm dry / broke
Example:
Estoy seco, pero igual salgo a gozar.
Translation:
I'm broke — but I still go out to enjoy.

Entry 42
No tengo ni pa'l pasaje
Vecina:
When you don't even have fare for the bus, "no tengo ni pa'l pasaje" is how we say you're completely broke —

you'll say it with swing and someone will still invite you to dance.

Meaning:

Don't even have for the fare

Example:

No tengo ni pa'l pasaje, toca caminar con flow.

Translation:

Not even enough for the fare — gotta walk with style.

Entry 43

Quedé limpio/a

Vecina:

After the party or the weekend, "quedé limpio/a" is the fun caleño way to say you spent everything but had a great time — you'll use this and everyone will laugh with you.

Meaning:

Left clean / with nothing

Example:

Después de la rumba quedé limpio, pero qué rico.

Translation:

After the party I was left with nothing — but so good.

Entry 44

Estoy en la olla

Vecina: When you're broke but still full of sabor, "estoy en la olla" is how we say it in Cali — you'll say it with a wink and the night keeps moving anyway.

Meaning:

I'm in the pot / broke

Example:

Estoy en la olla, pero la vida sigue sabrosa.

Translation:

I'm broke — but life keeps being tasty.

Entry 45

La plata voló

Vecina:

When the money disappears faster than a salsa turn, "la plata voló" is the caleño way to say it flew away — you'll say it laughing because the memories were worth it.

Meaning:

The money flew away

Example:

La plata voló en la rumba, qué vaina.

Translation:

The money flew away at the party — what a thing.

Entry 46

Ando corto/a

Vecina:

When you're short on cash but long on ganas, "ando corto/a" is how we say it with style — you'll use this and still buy a round for the crew.

Meaning:

I'm short on cash

Example:

Ando corto, pero igual invito un aguardiente.

Translation:

I'm short — but I'll still buy an aguardiente.

Entry 47

No hay con qué

Vecina:

When there's no money to do anything, "no hay con qué" is the honest caleño way to say it — you'll say it with rhythm and the party still finds a way.

Meaning:

There's nothing to work with

Example:

No hay con qué salir, pero hay con quién bailar.

Translation:

No money to go out — but there's someone to dance with.

Entry 48

Estoy pelado/a

Vecina:

When you're broke but still dressed to impress, "estoy pelado/a" is the caleño way to own it — you'll say it with swing and look richer than ever.

Meaning:

I'm broke / skinned

Example:

Estoy pelado, pero me visto sabroso igual.

Translation:

I'm broke — but I still dress tasty.

Entry 49
Sin un peso
Vecina:
When you have zero pesos but a heart full of rhythm, "sin un peso" is how we say it — you'll use this and the night will still feel rich.
Meaning:
Without a single peso
Example:
Sin un peso, pero con ganas de gozar.
Translation:
Without a single peso — but with desire to enjoy.

Entry 50
Estoy quebrado/a
Vecina:
When you're financially broken today but tomorrow the music plays again, "estoy quebrado/a" is the hopeful caleño way to say it — you'll say it and the salsa will fix everything.
Meaning:
I'm broken / ruined
Example:
Estoy quebrado, pero mañana bailo y se arregla.
Translation:
I'm broke — but tomorrow I dance and it fixes itself.

Carácter Caleño con Sabor

Real Caleño Character with Flavor

(Entries 51–60)

Entry 51

Ese man es un verraco

Vecina:

When someone is strong, sharp, and full of sabor, "ese man es un verraco" is how we say he's a beast — you'll drop this on the dance floor or in the street and everyone will nod with respect.

Meaning:

That guy is tough / impressive

Example:

Ese man es un verraco bailando, qué nivel.

Translation:

That guy is impressive dancing — what a level.

Entry 52

No se achica

Vecina:

When someone never shrinks or backs down, "no se achica" is the caleño way to say they stand tall — you'll use this and the whole group will feel the swing of real confidence.

Meaning:

Doesn't shrink / back down

Example:

No se achica en la pista, siempre al frente.

Translation:

Doesn't back down on the dance floor — always leading.

Entry 53

Tiene swing

Vecina:

When someone moves through life with natural rhythm and style, "tiene swing" is the highest caleño compliment — you'll say it and people will know they've got that Cali flow in their bones.

Meaning:

Has swing / rhythm

Example:

Tiene swing pa' bailar y pa' la vida.

Translation:

Has swing for dancing and for life.

Entry 54

Se para firme

Vecina:

When someone stands their ground with elegance and sabor, "se para firme" is how we say they don't flinch — you'll use this and the whole room will feel the strength behind the smile.

Meaning:

Stands firm

Example:
Se para firme en lo que quiere, con estilo.
Translation:
Stands firm in what he wants — with style.

Entry 55
Es un bacán
Vecina:
When someone is genuinely good-hearted and cool, "es un bacán" is the warm caleño way to say they're awesome — you'll drop this and the person will light up like a salsa turn.
Meaning:
He's awesome / great person
Example:
Es un bacán, siempre ayudando con sonrisa.
Translation:
He's awesome — always helping with a smile.

Entry 56
No se deja
Vecina:
When someone never lets anyone push them around but still does it with cariño, "no se deja" is the classy caleño way to say they set boundaries with heart.
Meaning:
Doesn't let himself be pushed
Example:
No se deja, pero lo dice con amor.

Translation:
Doesn't let himself be pushed — but says it with love.

Entry 57
Tiene su estilo
Vecina:
When someone has their own unique Cali flavor and walks with confidence, "tiene su estilo" is how we praise originality — you'll say it and the person will shine even brighter.
Meaning:
Has his own style
Example:
Tiene su estilo, siempre se ve rico.
Translation:
Has his style — always looks tasty.

Entry 58
Es pilas
Vecina:
When someone is sharp, alert, and never misses a beat, "es pilas" is the caleño way to say they're on point — you'll use this and the whole group will respect the energy.
Meaning:
He's sharp / alert
Example:
Es pilas, no se le pasa nada en la rumba.
Translation:

He's sharp — nothing slips by him at the party.

Entry 59
Se hace querer
Vecina:
When someone wins hearts without trying, "se hace querer" is how we say they're naturally endearing — you'll say it with a smile and the whole room will agree.
Meaning:
Makes himself loved / endearing
Example:
Se hace querer con esa sonrisa y ese baile.
Translation:
Makes himself loved with that smile and that dance.

Entry 60
Es un fiestero
Vecina:
When someone lives for the rumba and brings the joy, "es un fiestero" is the caleño way to say they're a true party soul — you'll use this and the night will feel even brighter.
Meaning:
He's a party person
Example:
Es un fiestero, siempre listo pa' gozar.
Translation:
He's a party person — always ready to enjoy.

Estado con Swing y Buena Vibra

Mood with Swing and Good Vibes

(Entries 61–70)

Entry 61

Estoy cansado pero contento

Vecina:

When the rumba was long but the heart is full, "estoy cansado pero contento" is how we say we're tired but smiling — you'll drop this after a night of salsa and everyone will understand the Caleño balance.

Meaning:

Tired but happy

Example:

Estoy cansado pero contento después de la rumba.

Translation:

Tired but happy after the party.

Entry 62

Me quedé sin batería

Vecina:

When the night drained you completely but you still want more tomorrow, "me quedé sin batería" is the fun caleño way to say you're out of energy — you'll say it with a laugh and the group will plan the next round.

Meaning:

I'm out of battery / drained

Example:

Me quedé sin batería, pero mañana volvemos.

Translation:

I'm out of battery — but tomorrow we go again.

Entry 63

Estoy en las nubes

Vecina:

When the music or the moment lifts you so high you're floating, "estoy en las nubes" is how we say we're on cloud nine — you'll use this on the dance floor and the whole room will feel your joy.

Meaning:

I'm on cloud nine

Example:

Con esa pareja estoy en las nubes.

Translation:

With that partner I'm on cloud nine.

Entry 64

Todo fluye

Vecina:

When life is moving smooth with good music and good company, "todo fluye" is the caleño way to say everything is flowing right — you'll say it and the night will feel even sweeter.

Meaning:

Everything flows

Example:
Cuando hay buena música todo fluye.
Translation:
When there's good music everything flows.

Entry 65
Estoy relajado/a
Vecina:
When you're truly at ease but still ready to move, "estoy relajado/a" is how we say we're relaxed with that Cali swing still in our bones — you'll use this while sipping a jugo and the vibe stays perfect.
Meaning:
I'm relaxed
Example:
Estoy relajado tomando un jugo en el parque.
Translation:
I'm relaxed having a juice in the park.

Entry 66
Me siento vivo/a
Vecina:
When the salsa or the city wakes you up again, "me siento vivo/a" is how we say we feel alive — you'll say it after a good song and the whole group will echo the same energy.
Meaning:
I feel alive
Example:

Con esta salsa me siento vivo otra vez.

Translation:

With this salsa I feel alive again.

Entry 67

Todo está rico

Vecina:

When the day or the night feels delicious all around, "todo está rico" is the sweetest caleño way to say everything is great — you'll use this and people will smile because they feel it too.

Meaning:

Everything is tasty / great

Example:

Todo está rico hoy, qué día tan bueno.

Translation:

Everything is tasty today — what a good day.

Entry 68

Estoy en mi salsa

Vecina:

When you're right in your element and the rhythm feels like home, "estoy en mi salsa" is the classic caleño way to say you're in your zone — nobody can stop you now.

Meaning:

I'm in my element

Example:

Cuando bailo estoy en mi salsa, nadie me para.

Translation:

When I dance, I'm in my element — no one stops me.

Entry 69
Me tiene contento/a
Vecina:
When something puts a real, big smile on your face, "me tiene contento/a" is the warm caleño way to say you're happy — you'll say it with that Cali glow and the party will shine brighter.
Meaning:
It's got me happy
Example:
El parche me tiene contenta, qué rico.
Translation:
The hangout has me happy — so nice.

Entry 70
Estoy que no quepo
Vecina:
When the joy is overflowing and you can't contain it, "estoy que no quepo" is how we say we're bursting — you'll use this on the dance floor and thc whole room will feel the explosion of happiness.
Meaning:
I can't contain it / overflowing
Example:
Con esta rumba estoy que no quepo.
Translation:

With this party I can’t contain it.

Cultura Vallecaucana que se Vive Bailando

Vallecaucana Culture That You Live Dancing (Entries 71–80)

Entry 71
Aquí todo es con sabor
Vecina:
Aquí en Cali todo viene con sabor — tú lo sientes en cada paso, en cada nota de salsa y en cada sonrisa que te dan en la calle.
Meaning:
Everything here has flavor / even calm has swing
Example:
Aquí todo es con sabor, hasta un café sabe diferente.
Translation:
Everything here has flavor — even a coffee tastes different.

Entry 72
Aquí la vida es tranquila
Vecina:
Aquí la vida es tranquila pero nunca aburrida — tú la vives con ritmo y te das cuenta que la calma caleña también tiene swing.
Meaning:

Life here is peaceful / but alive

Example:

Aquí la vida es tranquila, pero nunca aburrida.

Translation:

Life here is peaceful — but never boring.

Entry 73

Esto es pura alegría

Vecina:

Esto es pura alegría, de la que se siente en el pecho y se mueve con los pies — tú la vives en Cali y entiendes por qué la gente sonríe sin motivo.

Meaning:

This is pure joy / steady and unflashy

Example:

Este barrio es pura alegría, siempre hay música.

Translation:

This neighborhood is pure joy — there's always music.

Entry 74

Aquí la gente es querida

Vecina:

Aquí la gente es querida de verdad y eso se siente en cada abrazo y en cada "mi amor" que te dicen — tú lo notas y ya te sientes parte de la familia caleña.

Meaning:

Here people are beloved / that holds everything together

Example:

Aquí la gente es querida, todos se ayudan.

Translation:
Here people are loved — everyone helps each other.

Entry 75
Esto es de pura sabrosura
Vecina:
Esto es de pura sabrosura, no solo la comida sino la forma en que vivimos — tú lo pruebas y entiendes por qué en Cali todo sabe a fiesta.
Meaning:
Pure tastiness / flavorful way of life
Example:
La comida colombiana es de pura sabrosura, ¿no?
Translation:
Colombian food is pure deliciousness, right?

Entry 76
Aquí todo se goza
Vecina:
Aquí todo se goza, hasta un día de lluvia que te obliga a bailar en la sala — tú lo vives y empiezas a entender el verdadero sabor caleño.
Meaning:
Everything is enjoyed here / even the simple things
Example:
Aquí todo se goza, hasta un día de lluvia.
Translation:
Here everything is enjoyed — even a rainy day.

Entry 77
Esto es ritmo y corazón
Vecina:
Esto es ritmo y corazón, lo que nos define — tú lo sientes en cada paso de salsa y en cada abrazo que te dan en la calle.
Meaning:
Rhythm and heart / that defines a lot here
Example:
Colombia es ritmo y corazón, pura pasión.
Translation:
Colombia is rhythm and heart — pure passion.

Entry 78
Aquí todo tiene su tumbao
Vecina:
Aquí todo tiene su tumbao — hasta la forma de caminar por las calles de Cali — tú lo coges rápido y ya te mueves con ese swing que no se aprende en libros.
Meaning:
Everything has its tumbao / rhythmic swagger
Example:
Aquí todo tiene su tumbao, hasta caminar.
Translation:
Everything here has swagger — even walking.

Entry 79
Esto es vida sabrosa
Vecina:

Esto es vida sabrosa, no perfecta pero bien vivida con ritmo y corazón — tú la pruebas en Cali y ya no quieres vivirla de otra forma.

Meaning:

Tasty life / well-lived even if not perfect

Example:

Esto es vida sabrosa, con sus altos y bajos.

Translation:

This is a tasty life — with its ups and downs.

Entry 80

Aquí todo se vive bonito

Vecina:

Aquí todo se vive bonito, con cariño, con salsa y con ese sabor que solo Cali te da — tú lo sientes y te vas a casa con el corazón lleno.

Meaning: Everything is lived beautifully / understood here

Example:

Aquí todo se vive bonito, con cariño y sabor.

Translation:

Here everything is lived beautifully — with love and flavor.

Representative Glossary

(CS-04 – Caleño Flavor)

Chévere
Vecina:
The star word in Cali — you say "chévere" and you're already speaking with that warm, rhythmic caleño flavor that makes everything feel good.
Meaning:
Cool / great

Sabroso
Vecina:
When something feels delicious in every way — the music, the night, the moment — "sabroso" is how we say it in Cali, with swing and a smile.
Meaning:
Tasty / enjoyable

Mi rey / Mi reina
Vecina:
We call people "mi rey" or "mi reina" with affection, even strangers — you'll use this and instantly sound like you belong to the big Cali family.
Meaning:
My king / my queen (affectionate)

Flow
Vecina:
The rhythm you carry in your step and in your life — in Cali, having "flow" means you move with style, music, and natural sabor.
Meaning:
Rhythm / vibe / style

Rumba
Vecina:
The party, the night, the celebration — in Cali a rumba is never just a party, it's a feeling you dance with your whole soul.
Meaning:
Party

Swing
Vecina:
That special Cali groove you feel in your body when the music hits — having swing means you live life with rhythm and elegance.
Meaning:
Groove / style / rhythm

Gozar
Vecina:
To enjoy life fully, to savor every moment — in Cali we don't just live, we gozar, and we do it with heart and movement.

Meaning:
Enjoy / have fun

Sabor
Vecina:
The flavor, the essence, the soul of everything — in Cali we look for sabor in the music, the food, the people, and the way we live.
Meaning:
Flavor / essence

Verraco
Vecina:
When someone is impressive, strong, and full of talent, “verraco” is the highest caleño compliment — said with admiration and swing.
Meaning:
Tough / impressive / awesome

Bailar la vida
Vecina:
To dance through life instead of just walking it — this is the true Caleño philosophy: everything is better when you live it with rhythm.
Meaning:
Dance life / live with rhythm

Discover the Collection

The 8-Volume Series

Here's the full collection so you can keep exploring every corner of Colombia — from the mountains to the coast, without the fluff:

CS-01 – Colombian Slang for Brave Foreigners (National)
CS-02 – Paisa Slang for Brave Foreigners
CS-03 – Rolo Slang for Brave Foreigners
CS-04 – Caleño Slang for Brave Foreigners
CS-05 – Cafetero Slang for Brave Foreigners
CS-06 – Costeño Slang for Brave Foreigners
CS-07 – Santandereano & Boyacense Slang for Brave Foreigners
CS-08 – Pacific Coast Slang for Brave Foreigners

Acknowledgements

Gracias a toda mi gente caleña y vallecaucana que me enseñó a vivir con ritmo, con sabor y con el corazón bien grande. Gracias por las noches eternas de salsa, por los abrazos que aprietan, por las risas que se oyen desde la otra cuadra y por recordarme que en Cali la vida no se camina... se baila con swing y con toda el alma. ¡Esto es puro Cali, mi amor!

www.ingramcontent.com/pod-product-compliance
Lightning Source LLC
LaVergne TN
LVHW011052110826
845149LV00015B/3476

* 9 7 9 8 9 9 5 1 4 2 0 3 4 *